The Fountain

Karin Lessing

THE MONTEMORA FOUNDATION INC.
Box 336 Cooper Station
New York, N.Y.
10276

Some of these poems first appeared in *Montemora*, *Shearsman*, *Sulfur* and *Text*. "The Spaces of Sleep in Midsummer" was first published by Pentagram Press, Markesan, Wisconsin, in a limited letterpress edition.

The Fountain has been published as a special supplement to *Montemora*, a journal of international poetry and poetics, with support from NEA, CCLM and NYSCA.

The Montemora Foundation, Inc. is a non-profit, tax-exempt corporation devoted to international poetry and sponsored by donations and the sale of its publications.

Cover by Judy Fendelman.

Aquesta biua fuente que desseo
en este pan de vida yo la ueo
aůnque de noche.
   —*St. John of the Cross*

Se faire tout entier signe, c'est peut-être cela.
   —*E. Levinas*

TALISMAN

At the back of the head
a giant
anchors the eyelet sea:

in its jaw, a
bone
is singing: good fortune.

SHADOWS, FIRSTCOMERS...

Shadows, firstcomers,
sparked and feathered,
you fall, you
dive, driving the spar
into the lung's nest.

No angel, but a maypole,
from crown to
tip toe, swirling
ablaze. How
can the rootless ones
unlock this glow?

Breath, as it winds. I hear
the coronated
heart pod snap,
black, coruscant,
near.

LES SAINTES

Braced
the sea wall
and came, outcasts,

to the nacreous edge.

(How
each time we repeat

leaving our imprints,
our

cries: tellina, tellina).

•

Their salt robes
folded,

votive, on the
burning sand, even
the bottle caps.

The cave, too, burning.

To worship
upon the shore

Sara's
heart,

their shadowy pearl.

MORAINE

Through
thyme

braided
to thyme

followed
the scent that

tumbles,
breast-

high, dream-
thin.

Un-
thinking,

saw;
blinded,

heard
how they lie

cluster and
stray,

sometimes
seem to float.

NIGHT SONG

Cypress,

night's
needle, my

life's
slow gyre,

long night, long

dawn, the
star-
bristled day.

TURNING

Hollow
wood

where
are your rings on
rings: *white*

ripples *white.*
Years,

the bedded stream,
powers

as well as love,
spread

and almost touch.

•

Mountain,
veins
of beating

trace
apart, a-

part the

wind's sleeve

making
music to
a-
bide in.

THE SCULPTOR'S GARDEN

"it is as if they had destroyed beforehand
the words with which one might grasp them"

R.M. Rilke

Frost flowers
in the blaze.

The shattered, the a-
bandoned

grief looks out
sees

I remember, she says

river boats
playfully, the red
and gold drift

exposed,
love's children

(grass
devours wind, rain, time,
all
devouring),

wandering
the stones return

•

As if moss and lichen
were arms

retracting distances.

You,
among the innumerable,
shape loss

•

The work-bridge spins
itself in rust

at the garden's far edge: a
stone resembling sleep,

its
unfinished wing

•

PETROUS

How you skim and soar
over
the rainbow you
pull
feather by feather
out of the swollen air.

Quill-gifted,
ramified, the

flight's
structure.

The loss, the
gain: no wick to drain
your stone-
skinned sea.

You
never disembark.

LUBÉRON

In
your smouldering hip,
mountain,
searching your word:

again.

MINIATURE

Immensely,
your wrist,
     falconer

simple
as winds

flicks,
vaned,
toward prey

PRESAGE

Drained, the
deep blood cups
a thousand bees.

Damask. Your curtain, eye,
veils, reveals
the dreadful pattern.

Drink. The
indelible, once,
was your first rose.

LE BEAUCET: SHADOWS

Palaces, we
stray, through

one another
move.

Entrances, the
desolate stars,

o ridges
of Montmirail,
your jagged smile.

Follow her
wherever she walks, the

poem.

LIKE GLIDERS

in the wind
corridors

words
turn, re-

turn: listen,
watch them

and listen,
wave, their

wings
opening

toward sound,
out

over the pale
wreckage.

VIGIL

After the marriage
ceremony's
ingoing, outgoing,
rowing
of voices, vows —

the village *mairie*
like
some cinereous mushroom
of the heart's
intent,
casts off the lamps'
soft shadows.

Numb,
the dial,
the grooved fingers.

Night,
what drives
the brooding,
incessant voices
of love's passage:

night-rovers
circling, black-
ringed.

IL SOGNO DI CONSTANTINO

Dreamer,

your tent
dyed
amaranthine,

is rooted
brightness, the
small flower

each holds,
hand

touching
forehead,

as if
in that space
reflected,

endlessly
opening, all
echoes.

ANABATIC

Rock-
drift

high;
higher than

timber; the
heart-
line

stepped,
steps
beyond

towards
what
stone

wizened,
towards
whose

inaccessible
whirr.

WIND-GATHERED

Wind-gathered
      the tidal
air
—gathering
crests.

Nightbells'
alarm:

as many rooms as
tongues.

But from the
prairies' glitter
to the estuary:

the grain.

THE BARRIER

real, un-
real, a colored
flow,

that
explained the color,

but the rocks'
resonance—I still
hear it—

was more than
real.

tossing
the flowering
branch

"without aim or profit"

to see
its lightness, the

amazing
lightness,

grace
in being here

this side
of the oozing
rocks' resonance.

II

CÉZANNE

White-
washed the new

world of
cars willows

the moving things
we make move

through a savage
stillness — to

urge clay, the
beautiful

branched greens...
Watch,

where light
breaks, light's

arrow.

THESE

reeds: moon-
baskets, your

breath braided them,
cribbed a

dream,   Miriam

HER WORLD
for E.W.

Loosely, the
leaves 'my life

by water' by
air breath-fire and

earth the elemental
upturned boat-

room the simple
wildflowers'

perfect sounds.

FROM PLINY'S NATURAL HISTORY

drop
by drop

the favorite
wild, and

summer
myrrh

•

a handful, 'white
is purest'

says Pliny
cut

from root
to the strongest branches

twice
a year

•

tripartite, one
for the Sun

they drew lots
and the god's due

offered up,
lost;

sometimes
forests of cinnamon

ignite

•

JUNE POPPIES

June
poppies

flush
with the road

opening,
shutting,

the pine
mirrors

out
over the fields

the star-
braced shadows:

all
things

under a name

THROUGH GLASS

O, a baby's foot
hop-scotched
on flat tile
these flowerboxes
are tombs

·

Not clay,
desiccated
seed-cakes
currants delectable to Gauls—
that, now, from under
leaves   red
pearling through rock-cleft

·

Earth holds such secrets
that it would keep:
delicate bones
of an adolescent
girl in the womb's
clutches

·

Forget-me-not
that flower
to think, to
touch. . .
but colorless, to be racked
on that bed

outlasting
like clouds
or dreams   through glass

•

NEW OAK
for Nina

Eye-
vowel,
sheathed 'o'
of gold

golden lashes
under new
oak
leaf

the eye's
a pianino
light
plays on

moving
softly side-
ways

con-
sonant, as of color
itself.

ON THE WAY

Light then,
only the light   the summer's
last, cling to it.

See,
I'm radiant   and you,
holding it in, are

radiant...

Seeds
hum

Arcturus rises,   o you fire-
bearers, you

on the way to ice.

IMMORTELLES

sand
talking to sand

the unfrequent
words'

dunes

•

of this:
sight's fire
furled; a

sea
channelling
inwards

•

dreams'
secret

sun-
lit, lidded

tomb

•

. . . by shadow
to find

the twinned grain
paths

dwindling, a
whisper's

•

Orion's
moved, the

red-
shouldered hill

all wind-
keys

turning
in air

•

ANCESTRAL

rode.
rode you

black sails
from Odessa—

wind, a
toothful
of words

blown
inland,

o ashes: a

place, rock-
rooted,

hooves
to the sea, out

there, in no-
where's

white
white lashing.

DOLLS' HOUSES

I saw
through death's
little door

at Cartier's

the wizened tables, chairs, a
view

LAKEHURST, N.J.

"My name's
none of your biz"

she said, a
wilderness

gathering tracks, the
lost

scent, sea-
pine

BMT TROBAR

Our voices'
shreds

"strewn
all over hell

and gone," the
rag syllables

through air's
rings:

yours
was black, mine

vermilion

rose, swelling, breaking...

NAZCA

The smallest,
slightest, iridescent
bird, its wing, bill, claw

claws
at the petals'
overhang

these petals
are the gods'

they are
invisible to
men

•

Stones,
stones raked to
reveal lighter ground

making the
naked earth
visible
to the naked eye, saying

step in, step
in is to step out
of the world

•

absorbed
the essence

of claw, of
bill, wing, bird

I choose the
bird for it seems
most
perfect
among the patterns

the way
it imprints shape and
sound,

signalling, signalling the
gap,
flowery

food, drink, dance

•

The plane
glints
in the sun, spins out

in smoke-
tufted straights,
loops

'eternal
love, peace, days'

nor had earth
appeared
more beautiful in its ruins'

luminous web

    of sand, of
    stone, grass, wind.

THE IMAGE

Archer,
        hubbed

in the cloven
cove

to Samarkand:
your riches,

on trellises
of light:

the pomegranate
—my eye's—

suspended.

MIRROR

for Alexandra

You, Lady
with a
pearl, and

you, who
love such things:
ribbons

that curl, the
trickle

of white
acacia—you'd
root

breath's
blossom, thumb

and forefinger
gathering it, to

open, mirror,
your ermine-
edged,

breath-
less

gaze.

SEA-FOAM

to hear
again

the bird's
cry

pierce

pierce
and mend

•

leaf, a
knife,

a shadowy reef

blossom,

*Mer
de Chine*

•

where

sharp
and light

sails
of lobed breath

glide

•

your ridges'
blue, my

barest

news

•

even
the sun-
flower's

black
heart

reminds
me

love moves
also,

hate

•

that
from your lips

        it

never
    vanishes

grapes'
purple, sea's
dazzling

foam

    •

WHAT IT WANTS

endless, the
summer sky

darkening
at the edge, the hills

ride
on long shadows

cicada's
in the oak

something, what
is it it wants

wanting
it, grows

like stone
piled onto stone,

stylite,

through
the day

that, still
glittering,

grows

•

AIGUES MORTES

Half-blind, half-
seeing
look, there's
nowhere, its

gulls'
litter

where waves, once,
hugged
the puzzled
houses of dream

now walls, now
hushed, lid
upon lid,
captive, the

little waters
move—

ripening
in
its blindness, the
shelved salt

towers

•

THE BRIDGE

We entered
wrote ourselves

the runnels, the
white-wristed

bed
flowing under us

caught this, its
resonance

the wild, un-
spoken words'

troughs

•

as if lions
would keep, who,

whose
is there to

keep,
keep us from

grief, a
white

citadel
vanishes

•

though broken forth

I have no voice
to cry the season

the raging marble

the sun

    stained   hyacinth

Pont Flavien, 2 March 1980

SEPTEMBER-WINGS

A huge, soft
fire
comes

in pyramids
of leaves

days
flaked
with swallows

that austral
tug, all

under
Cassiopea's

steep
crown

•

skies'

scallop, black
lamp

of whistling

leaves

. . . .

not snow
      but swallows

the sudden
shining out of

things that
flock

dip to de-
ploy

taking us
somewhere

like a chime
rings on, then

quiets, the
un-

jewelled
void

•

NIKAIA

White bays
innumerable—

the creased
mirrors converge

to fold, hold
you,

caught
in their echoes,

Nike . . . fired

among lilies.

FONTAINE

I.

Eye to see sound, sound's
ear of

piled rocks   moss-headed

     these silences

to this, to
that

rock   tree
tree   rock

       to
covet   your white

voices

II.

black-
blown, springing

from bulb

big as a nail
big as skin
big as sky

hurled,
walking the
sky's

surge

•

into the echo-
web, lush

nest of
same   drawn

sisterly,

drone; the
wave

breaks, a
flutter

of seams
keeps

answering

•

al-
ways,

your voice, your in-
accessible
heart
in the crevasses.

Is it
breath
you want? Tongue,

its reeds,
pellets? Rain
fails.

Drink.
Drink from my snow-

fields.

•

III.

stood here
your hair
in leaves. as if

all
you'll never
know rose
to the edge. bleached,

ate
its way higher, each time,
then

dropped,
leaving its markings

only.
huge mouth, mouth
of the cave,
chasm, rock-

petalled
eye...would
purl, lash

the ruin-
risen

world   towards you.

CIRCE

She-
falcon's cry
circled: to

name   volcanoes
        name   seas

name islands   you'd
be that
rock
raging
alone.

   but the reeds'
lisp   the voices

of children
listing the road . . .

   •

byzantine, the
head tucked under
gold

tessarae   of place,
               speech,

unknown song   it changes
you could
not
grasp
it.

. . . whispered
among the reeds, reed-

comb fixed to the lay, eyes
all leaves

underfoot, the
stars, the subtle,
clandestine

here.

TERRA COTTA FIGURES, VILLA GIULIA

in memoriam D.H. Lawrence

from dark
chambered rock, wide-
eyed, bulb

through the bulbs'
painted door

what spring
steeved you to light, laid

its brightness
about you

•

anche il vento   even as wind

presses the leaf...

sunk, half
raised from clay, double-

fluted,
paired. as if they breathed
one another.

...on flowered stalks

•

                    was

    what leapt through
    your hands, un-

    still, plunging ever, wave-
                        seeded

    bronze,
    in your mirrors,

            the hills',

        wheat

    curved
    under.

PRIMAVERA

    papyrus   petals   dust
shredded, their bright clothes
    shrouds:

    there—nowhere else!—
white ruins   the brown fringed garland
    flung, un-

    written, *that* flash! and perilous
our own dying, much
    being born. Therefore

    she rises, green
foam   in which the hills are steeped
    and dawn

    feathery, your face
as I touched it   flown,
    nacreous, the doves'

    scooped
waves   I remember the
    first step taken, the dark glow—

    daughter
of,
    wind's pearl, *Primavera,*

then,
stepped on.

THE SPACES OF SLEEP IN MIDSUMMER

1.

floss, hirsute
angel   room

wide enough

to thread
through dormancy

dormancy and light

2.

a bowl, a mat of rushes   wind

                that rock-
scooper, extravagant

rose

3.

of dawn's
blank sweepings

I speak

    the feral plain

4.

no matter which way you
turn, out-
ward,

into the sea of darkness

                  words,
these scantlings

5.

conch-
shell, a candle

for furnishings

bread,
    that the tree would last

a mouth-
ful
crumbles, o earth

6.

carry me, I'd go
to the edge   of chagrin

leaf-tip   horizon

sea-
green, where it blows

mirror eddying out. tethered

mirage

7.

that it drives, that it
unclenches

snake, I
fable myself

from lavender
to lavender

clasped, the crescent   oils

8.

crow-
shadow,
chandelier

the spaces
of sleep

the spaces of
sleep in midsummer

grow
through my hands

vines,
vines branched

towards thunder

•